Creative Cooking with Oats

HEARTY BANANA OAT FLAPJACKS

2 large ripe bananas, peeled and sliced

1 tablespoon granulated sugar

1 cup all-purpose flour

1/2 cup Quaker® Oats (quick or old fashioned, uncooked)

1 tablespoon baking powder

1/4 teaspoon ground cinnamon

1/4 teaspoon salt (optional)

1 cup fat-free (skim) milk

1 egg, lightly beaten

2 tablespoons vegetable oil

Aunt Jemima® Syrup, warmed

Additional banana slices (optional)

Coarsely chopped pecans or walnuts (optional)

1. Combine banana slices and sugar in medium bowl; stir to coat slices with sugar. Set aside.

2. Combine flour, oats, baking powder, cinnamon and salt, if desired, in large bowl; mix well. Combine milk, egg and oil in medium bowl; blend well. Add to dry ingredients all at once; stir just until dry ingredients are moistened. (Do not overmix.)

3. Heat griddle over medium-high heat (or preheat electric skillet or griddle to 375°F). Lightly grease griddle. For each pancake, pour scant 1/4 cup batter onto hot griddle. Top with four or five sugar-coated banana slices. Turn pancakes when tops are covered with bubbles and edges look cooked.

4. Serve with warm syrup and additional banana slices and nuts, if desired.

Makes 12 (4-inch) pancakes

DOUBLE ORANGE WALNUT MUFFINS

1¹/₂ cups all-purpose flour*

  1 cup **Quaker® Oats** (quick or old fashioned, uncooked)

²/₃ cup plus 1 tablespoon granulated sugar, divided

  2 teaspoons baking powder

¹/₂ teaspoon baking soda

¹/₄ teaspoon salt

³/₄ cup coarsely chopped toasted walnuts,** divided

²/₃ cup plus ¹/₄ cup **Tropicana Pure Premium®** orange juice, divided

¹/₂ cup low-fat (1%) or fat-free (skim) milk

  1 large egg

¹/₄ cup (¹/₂ stick) butter or margarine, melted and cooled

If using old fashioned oats, add 2 tablespoons additional flour.

**To toast walnuts, spread in single layer in heavy-bottomed skillet. Cook over medium heat 1 to 2 minutes, stirring frequently, until nuts are lightly browned. Remove from skillet immediately. Cool before using.*

1. Heat oven to 400°F. Line 12 medium muffin cups with paper baking cups or spray bottoms only with nonstick cooking spray.

2. Stir together flour, oats, ²/₃ cup sugar, baking powder, baking soda and salt in large bowl. Add ¹/₂ cup walnuts; mix well. Set aside. Beat ²/₃ cup juice, milk, egg and butter with whisk or fork in medium bowl until well blended. Add to dry ingredients all at once; stir just until dry ingredients are moistened. (Do not overmix.)

3. Pour into muffin cups, dividing evenly. Sprinkle tops with remaining ¹/₄ cup walnuts.

4. Bake 15 to 18 minutes or until wooden pick inserted in centers comes out clean. Remove pan from oven and immediately spoon remaining ¹/₄ cup orange juice over muffin tops, dividing evenly. Let stand 5 minutes. Sprinkle muffin tops with remaining 1 tablespoon sugar. Remove from pan. Serve warm.

Makes 12 muffins

Tip: Chopped toasted pecans may be substituted for walnuts. Nuts may be omitted, if desired.

APPLE BERRY BREAKFAST CRISP

FILLING

4 cups thinly sliced peeled apples (about 4 medium)

2 cups fresh or frozen blueberries or sliced strawberries

1/4 cup firmly packed brown sugar

1/4 cup frozen orange juice concentrate, thawed

2 tablespoons all-purpose flour

1 teaspoon ground cinnamon

TOPPING

1 cup **Quaker® Oats** (quick or old fashioned, uncooked)

1/2 cup firmly packed brown sugar

1/3 cup (5 tablespoons plus 1 teaspoon) margarine or butter, melted

2 tablespoons all-purpose flour

1. Heat oven to 350°F. Spray 8-inch square glass baking dish with nonstick cooking spray. For filling, combine apples, blueberries, brown sugar, juice concentrate, flour and cinnamon in large bowl; stir until fruit is evenly coated. Spoon into baking dish.

2. For topping, combine oats, brown sugar, margarine and flour in medium bowl; mix until crumbly. Sprinkle evenly over fruit.

3. Bake 30 to 35 minutes or until apples are tender. Serve warm.

Makes 9 servings

Tip: For a delicious dessert, serve warm with vanilla frozen yogurt.

ORANGE CRANBERRY OATMEAL

2 cups **Tropicana Pure Premium**® orange juice

1 cup water

1/4 teaspoon salt

1/8 teaspoon ground cinnamon

2 cups **Quaker**® **Oats** (quick or old fashioned, uncooked)

1/2 cup dried cranberries

1 cup low-fat or fat-free vanilla yogurt

1/4 cup chopped toasted walnuts*

Additional dried cranberries (optional)

To toast walnuts, spread in single layer in heavy-bottomed skillet. Cook over medium heat 1 to 2 minutes, stirring frequently, until nuts are lightly browned. Remove from skillet immediately. Cool before using.

1. Bring orange juice, water, salt and cinnamon to a gentle boil in medium saucepan. Stir in oats and cranberries. Return to a boil; reduce heat to medium. Cook 1 minute for quick oats, 5 minutes for old fashioned oats or until most of liquid is absorbed, stirring occasionally. Let stand until desired consistency.

2. Spoon oatmeal into four cereal bowls. Top each serving with 1/4 cup yogurt, 1 tablespoon walnuts and additional cranberries, if desired.

Makes 4 servings

Microwave Directions: Combine all ingredients except yogurt and nuts in 3-quart microwaveable bowl. Microwave on HIGH 4 to 6 minutes for quick oats and 7 to 9 minutes for old fashioned oats or until most of the liquid is absorbed. Let stand until desired consistency. Top each serving with yogurt, walnuts and additional cranberries, if desired.

HEARTY MEATBALL STEW

1   pound ground turkey breast or extra-lean ground beef

³/₄   cup **Quaker® Oats** (quick or old fashioned, uncooked)

1   can (8 ounces) no-salt-added tomato sauce, divided

1¹/₂ teaspoons garlic powder

1¹/₂ teaspoons dried thyme leaves, divided

2   cans (14¹/₂ ounces each) 70% less sodium, fat-free chicken broth

³/₄   teaspoon salt (optional)

¹/₃   cup ditalini or other small pasta

2¹/₂ cups any frozen vegetable blend (do not thaw)

¹/₄   cup water

2   tablespoons cornstarch

1. Heat broiler. Lightly spray rack of broiler pan with nonstick cooking spray.

2. Combine turkey, oats, ¹/₃ cup tomato sauce, garlic powder and 1 teaspoon thyme in large bowl; mix lightly but thoroughly. Transfer to sheet of aluminum foil or waxed paper. Pat mixture into 9×6-inch rectangle. Cut into 1¹/₂-inch squares; roll each square into a ball. Arrange meatballs on broiler pan.

3. Broil meatballs 6 to 8 inches from heat about 6 minutes or until cooked through, turning once.

4. While meatballs cook, bring broth, remaining tomato sauce, remaining ¹/₂ teaspoon thyme and salt, if desired, to a boil in 4-quart saucepan or Dutch oven over medium-high heat. Add pasta and vegetables; return to a boil. Reduce heat; cover and simmer 10 minutes or until pasta and vegetables are tender. Stir together water and cornstarch in small bowl until smooth. Add to pan along with meatballs. Cook and stir until broth is thickened. Spoon into bowls.

Makes 6 servings

SAUCY STUFFED PEPPERS

  6 medium green bell peppers

1¼ cups water

  2 cups low-sodium tomato juice, divided

  1 can (6 ounces) tomato paste

  1 teaspoon dried oregano leaves, divided

½ teaspoon dried basil leaves

½ teaspoon garlic powder, divided

  1 pound lean ground beef

1½ cups **Quaker® Oats** (quick or old fashioned, uncooked)

  1 medium tomato, chopped

¼ cup chopped carrot

¼ cup chopped onion

1. Heat oven to 350°F. Cut bell peppers lengthwise in half; remove membranes and seeds. Set aside.

2. For sauce, combine water, 1 cup tomato juice, tomato paste, ½ teaspoon oregano, basil and ¼ teaspoon garlic powder in medium saucepan over medium heat. Simmer 10 to 15 minutes. Set aside.

3. For filling, combine beef, oats, tomato, carrot and onion with remaining 1 cup tomato juice, remaining ½ teaspoon oregano and ¼ teaspoon garlic powder in large bowl, mixing lightly but thoroughly.

4. Fill each bell pepper half with about ⅓ cup meat mixture. Place in 13×9-inch glass baking dish; pour reserved sauce evenly over bell peppers. Bake 45 to 50 minutes to medium doneness (160°F) until not pink in center and juices show no pink color.

Makes 12 servings

SPICY OAT-CRUSTED CHICKEN WITH SUNSHINE SALSA

SUNSHINE SALSA

3/4 cup prepared salsa

3/4 cup coarsely chopped orange sections

CHICKEN

2 tablespoons canola oil

1 tablespoon margarine, melted

2 teaspoons chili powder

1 teaspoon garlic powder

1 teaspoon ground cumin

3/4 teaspoon salt

1 1/2 cups **Quick Quaker® Oats**, uncooked

1 egg, lightly beaten

1 tablespoon water

4 boneless, skinless chicken breast halves (about 5 to 6 ounces each)

Chopped cilantro (optional)

1. Combine salsa and orange sections in small bowl. Cover and chill.

2. Heat oven to 375°F. Line baking sheet with aluminum foil. Stir together oil, margarine, chili powder, garlic powder, cumin and salt in flat, shallow dish. Add oats, stirring until evenly moistened.

3. Beat egg and water with fork until frothy in second flat, shallow dish. Dip chicken into egg mixture, then coat completely in seasoned oats. Place chicken on foil-lined baking sheet. Pat any extra oat mixture onto top of chicken.

4. Bake 30 minutes or until chicken is cooked through and oat coating is golden brown. Serve with Sunshine Salsa. Garnish with cilantro, if desired.

Makes 4 servings

VEGGIE BURGERS

3 teaspoons vegetable oil, divided

1 cup sliced mushrooms

1 cup shredded carrots (about 2)

3/4 cup chopped onion (about 1 medium)

3/4 cup chopped zucchini (about 1 small)

2 cups **Quaker® Oats** (quick or old fashioned, uncooked)

1 can (15 ounces) kidney beans, rinsed and drained

1 cup cooked white or brown rice

2 tablespoons soy sauce or 1/2 teaspoon salt

1 teaspoon minced garlic

1/8 teaspoon black pepper

1/2 cup chopped fresh cilantro or chives (optional)

Hamburger buns and toppings (optional)

1. Heat 1 teaspoon oil in large nonstick skillet. Add mushrooms, carrots, onions and zucchini; cook over medium-high heat 5 minutes or until vegetables are tender.

2. Transfer vegetables to food processor bowl. Add oats, beans, rice, soy sauce, garlic, pepper and cilantro, if desired. Pulse for about 20 seconds or until well blended. Divide into eight 1/2-cup portions. Shape into patties between waxed paper. Refrigerate at least 1 hour or until firm.

3. Heat remaining 2 teaspoons oil in same skillet over medium-high heat. Cook patties 3 to 4 minutes on each side or until golden brown. Serve on buns with toppings, if desired.

Makes 8 servings

MEATLOAF FOCACCIA SANDWICH

SPREAD

1 ounce sun-dried tomatoes (not in oil)

1/2 cup fat-free or reduced-fat mayonnaise

1 clove garlic, minced

Dash hot pepper sauce

MEATLOAF

1 1/2 pounds lean ground beef or ground turkey breast

3/4 cup **Quaker® Oats** (quick or old fashioned, uncooked)

1/2 cup thinly sliced green onions

1/2 cup fat-free (skim) milk

1 egg, lightly beaten

1 teaspoon dried thyme leaves

1 teaspoon salt

1/2 teaspoon black pepper

SANDWICH FIXINGS

1 loaf focaccia bread, about 8×10 inches in diameter (about 1 1/2 pounds)

8 slices reduced-fat Swiss or part-skim mozzarella cheese

8 large lettuce leaves

1. Heat oven to 350°F. For spread, soften tomatoes according to package directions; coarsely chop. Combine tomatoes, mayonnaise, garlic and hot pepper sauce in small bowl; mix well. Cover and chill.

2. For meatloaf, combine beef, oats, green onions, milk, egg, thyme, salt and pepper in large bowl; mix lightly but thoroughly. Press mixture evenly into 9×5-inch metal loaf pan.

3. Bake 60 to 75 minutes or until meatloaf is medium doneness and center is no longer pink (160°F for beef; 170°F for turkey). Drain off any juices. Let stand 5 minutes before slicing.

4. To serve, cut focaccia into 8 rectangles; cut each rectangle in half horizontally. Spread 1 tablespoon spread on inside surfaces of each focaccia piece. Cut meatloaf into 8 slices; place on half of focaccia rectangles. Top with cheese and lettuce; cover with remaining pieces of focaccia. Serve warm.

Makes 8 servings

ASIN STUFFED MUSHROOMS

24 large mushrooms (about 2 pounds)

1/2 cup reduced-sodium soy sauce

1/4 cup dry sherry

1/2 pound ground turkey

3/4 cup **Quaker® Oats** (quick or old fashioned, uncooked)

1/2 cup sliced green onions

1/4 cup finely chopped red or green bell pepper

1 egg white, lightly beaten

1 tablespoon Dijon-style mustard

2 cloves garlic, minced

1. Remove stems from mushrooms; reserve stems. Place mushroom caps in large bowl. Combine soy sauce and sherry in small bowl; pour over mushrooms. Cover and marinate at least 1 hour, stirring once after 30 minutes.

2. Finely chop reserved mushroom stems. Place in large bowl with turkey, oats, green onions, bell pepper, egg white, mustard and garlic; mix well. Drain mushroom caps, reserving marinade. Fill caps with turkey mixture, packing well and mounding slightly. Place on broiler pan. Brush tops with reserved marinade.

3. Broil 7 to 8 inches from heat 15 to 18 minutes or until turkey is cooked through. Serve immediately.

*Makes **24** appetizers*

QUAKER'S BEST OATMEAL BREAD

5³/₄ to 6¹/₄ cups all-purpose flour

2¹/₂ cups **Quaker® Oats** (quick or old fashioned, uncooked)

¹/₄ cup granulated sugar

2 packages (¹/₄ ounce each) quick-rising yeast (about 4¹/₂ teaspoons)

2¹/₂ teaspoons salt

1¹/₂ cups water

1¹/₄ cups fat-free (skim) milk

¹/₄ cup (¹/₂ stick) margarine or butter

1. Combine 3 cups flour, oats, sugar, yeast and salt in large bowl; mix well. Heat water, milk and margarine in small saucepan until very warm (120°F to 130°F). Add to flour mixture. Blend with electric mixer on low speed until dry ingredients are moistened. Increase to medium speed; beat 3 minutes. By hand, gradually stir in enough remaining flour to make stiff dough.

2. Turn dough out onto lightly floured surface. Knead 5 to 8 minutes or until smooth and elastic. Shape dough into ball; place in greased bowl, turning once. Cover; let rise in warm place 30 minutes or until doubled in size.

3. Punch down dough. Cover; let rest 10 minutes. Divide dough in half; shape to form loaves. Place in two greased 8×4-inch or 9×5-inch loaf pans. Cover; let rise in warm place 15 minutes or until nearly doubled in size.

4. Heat oven to 375°F. Bake 45 to 50 minutes or until dark golden brown. Remove from pans to wire rack. Cool completely before slicing.

Makes 2 loaves (32 servings)

Tip: If desired, brush tops of loaves lightly with melted margarine or butter and sprinkle with additional oats after placing in pans.

SOFT OATY PRETZELS

3 to 3½ cups all-purpose flour, divided

1½ cups **Quaker® Oats** (quick or old fashioned, uncooked), divided

2 tablespoons granulated sugar

1 package (¼ ounce) quick-rising yeast (about 2¼ teaspoons)

1½ teaspoons salt

¾ cup milk

¾ cup water

2 tablespoons margarine or butter, softened

1 egg, lightly beaten

1. Combine 2 cups flour, 1¼ cups oats, sugar, yeast and salt in large bowl; mix well. Heat milk and water in small saucepan until very warm (120°F to 130°F); stir in margarine. Add to flour mixture. Blend with electric mixer at low speed until moistened; beat 3 minutes at medium speed. By hand, gradually stir in enough remaining flour to make soft dough that pulls away from sides of bowl.

2. Turn dough out onto lightly floured surface. Knead 5 to 8 minutes or until smooth and elastic, adding additional flour if dough is sticky. Cover loosely with plastic wrap; let dough rest on floured surface 10 minutes.

3. Heat oven to 350°F. Lightly grease or spray two large baking sheets with nonstick cooking spray.

4. Divide dough into 24 equal pieces. Roll each piece into 12-inch-long rope; form into pretzel, letter or number shape. Place on baking sheet. Cover loosely with plastic wrap; let rest 10 minutes or until slightly risen. Brush tops of pretzel with beaten egg; sprinkle with remaining ¼ cup oats, pressing lightly.

5. Bake 15 to 18 minutes or until golden brown. (If baking both sheets at one time, rotate sheets top to bottom and front to back halfway through baking time.) Remove from baking sheets; cool on wire racks. Store tightly covered at room temperature.

Makes 24 pretzels

BERRY BERRY STREUSEL BARS

1^1/$_2$ cups **Quaker® Oats** (quick or old fashioned, uncooked)

1^3/$_4$ cups all-purpose flour

^{1}/$_2$ cup firmly packed brown sugar

^{3}/$_4$ cup (1^1/$_2$ sticks) butter or margarine, melted

1 cup fresh or frozen blueberries (do not thaw)

^{1}/$_3$ cup raspberry or strawberry preserves

1 teaspoon all-purpose flour

^{1}/$_2$ teaspoon grated lemon peel (optional)

1. Heat oven to 350°F.

2. Combine oats, flour, brown sugar and butter; mix until crumbly. Reserve 1 cup oat mixture for topping. Set aside. Press remaining mixture onto bottom of ungreased 8- or 9-inch square baking pan. Bake 13 to 15 minutes or until light golden brown. Cool slightly.

3. Combine blueberries, preserves, flour and lemon peel, if desired, in medium bowl; mix gently. Spread over crust. Sprinkle with reserved oat mixture, patting gently.

4. Bake 20 to 22 minutes or until light golden brown. Cool completely. Cut into bars. Store tightly covered.

Makes 15 bars

CHEWY CHOCOLATE NO-BAKES

1 cup semisweet chocolate chips

5 tablespoons light butter

14 large marshmallows

1 teaspoon vanilla

2 cups **Quaker® Oats** (quick or old fashioned, uncooked)

²/₃ cup (any combination of) raisins, diced dried mixed fruit, shredded coconut, miniature marshmallows or chopped nuts

1. Melt chocolate chips, butter and large marshmallows in large saucepan over low heat, stirring until smooth. Remove from heat; cool slightly. Stir in vanilla. Stir in oats and remaining ingredients.

2. Drop by rounded tablespoonfuls onto waxed paper. Cover and refrigerate 2 to 3 hours. Let stand at room temperature about 15 minutes before serving. Store tightly covered in refrigerator.

Makes about 36 treats

Microwave directions: Place chocolate chips, butter and marshmallows in large microwaveable bowl. Microwave on HIGH (100% power) 1 to 2 minutes or until mixture is melted and smooth, stirring every 30 seconds. Proceed as recipe directs.